Party of One

Bereaved or Relieved?

by
Maria A. Abbott

PublishAmerica
Baltimore

© 2009 by Maria A. Abbott.
All rights reserved. No part of this book may be reproduced, stored in a retrieval system or transmitted in any form or by any means without the prior written permission of the publishers, except by a reviewer who may quote brief passages in a review to be printed in a newspaper, magazine or journal.

First printing

PublishAmerica has allowed this work to remain exactly as the author intended, verbatim, without editorial input.

ISBN: 1-60836-136-5
PUBLISHED BY PUBLISHAMERICA, LLLP
www.publishamerica.com
Baltimore

Printed in the United States of America

*To my daughter,
Dr Clydette Powell,
who believes I could climb
Mt Everest wearing flip-flops….*

Acknowledgments

The following people helped me with some aspect of this book: Dr. Clydette Powell, Dr. John Woods, Taryn Vian, Gay Harrington, Dominique Pickett, Mike Gower, Junia Dantas, Mariza de Paula, Ellen Roberts, Sandra Phaup, an unnamed woman at The Shakespeare Theater, Goodwin House Retirement Community, Arlington Central Library, Milton and Lydia Hernandez, all the widows interviewed who were so willing to tell their stories, and many others who encouraged me along the way.

Table of Contents

Introduction 11
Up, Up and Away! 14
Draw Your Own Blueprints! 21
Biblically Incorrect 25
Bookends 30
Caramel 34
Dynamite 39
The Galaxy Is Yours 45
Is Happiness East of Here? 50
La Vie Est Breve 55
Love at Any Age 59
The Rings Kept Their Promise 63
Out of Her Shell 70
The Silent Explosion 74
Tale of Two Widows 78
Three Ships 82
Whose Choice Is It? 90
Death of a Marriage 94
Annex 99

Party of One

Bereaved or Relieved?

Introduction

What do widows have in common? One thing—the loss of their husbands—though nothing else. Some widows are outright relieved that their husband went away for ever, due to a variety of reasons. A few widows are unhappy for the rest of their lives. Their function in life has been taken away, as they are no longer the Mrs, the better half, nurse, nanny, or other label pinned on them by society. With their significance gone, they wonder what they will now do. They feel lost.

After interviewing over fifty widows from diverse backgrounds, I reached the conclusion that the majority of widows go on to live productive and successful lives on their own, making a difference in the world, with neither encouragement nor ridicule from their husband had he been alive. In fact, it is astonishing to identify the number of merry widows and the reasons for their delight. On the other hand, a few of the ones I interviewed were profoundly saddened without the love of their lives. They depended on them emotionally as well practically, for day-to-day living. These widows had lost their hope. They stayed interminably cheerless, almost seeming to enjoy their grief. Everyone felt sorry for them and praised them for their bravery in getting up each morning, though for that widow it was only to endure another twenty four hours of despair.

Those who did not endlessly grieve were an intriguing group of women. They didn't feel sorry for themselves for two reasons. Either their husband had suffered a prolonged illness, and she was relieved to see his torment end; or, they had experienced dismal marriages which overflowed with unresolved problems. Death compassionately brought tranquility and closing to an intolerable situation. Destiny made a grand and swift appearance, liberating everybody. No questions asked. The end!

Widowhood, welcomed or not, has its closure. In contrast, divorce is more difficult and the story of that relationship doesn't end on the day the final papers are signed. The ex-husband is still around in the world somewhere, and oftentimes uncomfortably near by. Children have to be considered, alimony paid, division of properties negotiated, plus all the uneasy occasions when both natural parents have to attend events, such as christenings, graduations, weddings, and family reunions. When both exes have remarried, the situation is cumbersome at best.

Moreover, in cases of divorce, the wife is frequently blamed for the break-up. Everybody loves and mourns for the widow, but the divorcee is not allocated the same kind of compassion. Yet, what about the ex-husband? Was he always the innocent party? Did he, while married but in the throes of a mid-life crisis, go off hunting for a younger, more exciting wife, and then the marriage died, leaving a married "widow"?

From these fifty-some interviews, I have chosen life stories that illustrate the various pathways that widows may take. I begin with how the couple met, how their life together evolved, and what transpired in the relationship as the husband became sick and died. I then trace how the widow adapted to her new life alone—as the "party of one"—and how she viewed herself (whether bereaved or relieved) and what she did to define her future as a single person again. Although all the stories are based on real life interviews, I have taken a story as illustrative and adapted some aspects to protect the identity of the person interviewed, while preserving the essence of the real life account. Some life stories generate life lessons that are applicable across cultures and time.

If you are a widow reading this book, consider where your life parallels these stories and where you fit in. What are your innermost thoughts when you stand in front of the bathroom mirror in a haze after a night's sleep and take one good, long look inside yourself? Do you ask, "Am I genuinely bereaved, or secretly relieved? Do I fit into one perspective, or to the other?" On the other hand, if you are not a widow, what elements of the story reflect your current situation? Are there patterns in the life stories that might reveal important components of your relationship and your identity? If you were to outlive your partner, what course of life would you take? Would you stay on the same road, or would your life take a different turn?

Widows, merry or otherwise, unite. You're not alone. Life is out there waiting for your new beginning. Go!

Up, Up and Away!

A serene retirement community where every day resembled the day before and the one after. Peace uninterrupted, other than an occasional rumble when someone passed on and everyone went to the memorial service, gratefully thanking God that it was not their turn...not yet.

Trips to the "pillary" (where they got their daily allowance of drugs) were part of the routine, a somewhat electrifying moment. Without their pills they would run the chance of being the next one to be memorialized at the chapel. Their Maker would just have to wait a little longer. No one was really quite ready.

Meanwhile life went on...almost unbearably tranquil...with one exception. The few men living there stumbled around, grabbing on to walkers or whirling their wheel chairs in the halls were all after a certain resident. What a remarkable beauty she was! Age had not damaged her perfect face and figure. She was the envy of the entire population of that comfortable world, exciting enough to keep many men almost loosing their minds but keeping their bodies in good shape, just in case! Who knew when she would succumb? Who would finally conquer her? The chase never ended. These guys were like adolescents in love hoping for a fleeting glance, a word, a brush of the hand from that exquisite princess. Like sick puppies in love, the men returned to their rooms every night and dreamed about her. During quiet moments of the day they fantasized about their future. Who would finally gain her affection and live happily ever after?

This pursuit continued, they often tripped in the process, this was an exhausting activity for the octogenarians but excellent for their heart beats. No clogged arteries in that bunch. The prospect of the "prize catch" kept them alive and filled with blissful anticipation…building castles in the air, never missing a trip to the "pill gourmet" for their daily medications. Health and agility were a must. A competition was happening, and stamina had to be maintained at any cost!

Her youth was busy. Following World War II, she worked for the occupation forces in Japan—an accomplishment beyond all normal aspects for this Bostonian debutante. Her mother did not approve of her moving to the Far East to hold a common job. It was demeaning for a young lady from a refined, upper class New England family to go away from her home town and be a secretary, taking orders from some ordinary soldier. The daughter applied for positions overseas, and correspondence with invitations for interviews was sent to her address. Her mother secretly discarded the letters hoping that her "little girl" would change her mind. This must have been a passing fancy in the immature brain of such a youngster. Imagine leaving home for some harsh adventuresome existence in post war Tokyo! This was not only unthinkable but most likely dangerous…not her daughter. Heaven forbid!

One day unbeknownst to her mother, a letter slipped through, followed by a phone call and a job offer. A short while later arrangements were quickly and quietly made, and the young lady was ready to head west to Seattle to fly over the Pacific...all this before the mother could possibly be aware of the events taking place. The beginning of a new life! No more motherly advice, no more loving supervision. She was liberated, soaring around her own skies, testing her brand new wings. Visions of a mystifying bright future awaited her!

During that era it took many weeks to sail to Japan from the U.S. Had her mother not thrown away all the initial letters with job offers, she would have traveled to Yokohama, a four-week ocean voyage crossing through the Panama Canal...a dreamy holiday aboard a ship. Oh well she mused, she was independent at last and she might opt to return by passenger liner and be invited to sip champagne at the Captain's table!

Once arriving at her destination, she began her secretarial duties right away working for an Army officer. The department had only two other women surrounded by twenty handsome bachelors. A haven for single "girls". Potential husbands were all around, all of them successful and looking for wives. What could be better? She would do her parents proud, perhaps someday arriving home arm in arm married to a decorated war hero with a chest covered with medals. He would be the star of family reunions, and she would sparkle with delight and pride!

Life went on as usual in the office and everyone toiled diligently, happy to be away from the watchful eyes of dedicated parents. During off hours there were many parties, dances, picnics, and a lot of fun with boys overseas. Some of the men were conveniently absent minded forgetting abut their marriages back in The States…and everyone had a whale of a good time.

After several months of carefree survival, which was quickly becoming a way of life, the magical day arrived. The man of her dreams appeared in front of her…bells rang and birds sang! An immediate attraction burst out in the air! An extremely good looking hunk of Arab-American heritage. Tall, slim, sun tanned with deep blue eyes and oozing with charm and poise. A wonder of wonders that had our proper Bostonian young lady weak at the knees. She did not let on right away, why not pretend for a while? He was after all a "foreigner", charismatic but still out of her league. An Arab, goodness, what would her family think? It was bad enough that she had to meet him in the Far East, but now a Bedouin too? Her Puritan ancestors would go into complete disbelief and shock.

After going out with him and falling utterly in love with him and he with her, the legendary day came. He proposed marriage. She hesitantly, daintily, properly, and rapidly said "oh, yes!" Off they went on with a blissful life. They were quite compatible despite the differences in backgrounds. Once the family recuperated from the astonishing news, they quieted down to mere prayers and whispers that this event would not be the disappointment of a lifetime for their only daughter.

The couple was married for 50 years and had two gorgeous girls, the perfect blend of Bedouin-Boston features. Life in Japan was comfortable and easy. They lived in a large house with the view of Mount Fuji. A wonderful spot with all the conveniences offered to officers and their families. Life was blissful

In her imagination the Panama Canal still loomed as one of the world's wonders and crossing it aboard a ship was a dream that lingered on…since the day when she was called to work late and missed waving good bye to friends who were sailing home on that amazing voyage. Her devoted husband right then and there decided to make her dream come true and book passage on a ship in preparation for their return to the U.S. The day of their departure she was beside herself with excitement. The trip of a life time between two oceans, absolute heaven! All through the crossing he was his usual charming self, full of zest and good humor. Other passengers looked on at this sparkling couple whizzing through the dance floor. Love was all around and blooming. It was so exciting almost as though it was their last hurrah, the last fling on the high seas!

Fortunate and poignant as the same time, destiny was about to deal them a shock that would part them for ever. After being home for some weeks he began to mention he was not up to his usual energy and not feeling well in general. He was taken to a doctor who immediately checked him into a nearby hospital for further testing. He never came home. He was dead in a matter of days….suddenly, with no serious warning. What an enormous and overwhelming shock for his wife and children! She was enveloped in a feeling of utter loss, confusion and grief. Life became unbearable. She was alone, and he had always been such help and support for her. Now she had to handle it unaided. All this was perplexing and chaotic.

She simply had to come to terms with these circumstances and go forward on her own. Through determination and faith in the future, she managed to keep her good sense. For the sake of the family and her pride, she slowly succeeded through the endless road, step-by-step.

After a few months, she resolved to look for a small house. She had to leave the big one where they lived, filled with memories that would not disappear, ever. Those memories brought sadness, joys, and longings for the happy days they shared together. In her search for a new home, she happened to find a retirement community filled with people who welcomed her with open arms. What a treasure she had discovered! Great company, attractive surroundings, delicious food and to keep her heart and mind occupied—a myriad of activities. Not another lonely moment in sight.

Her only problem was the suitors, not that she considered that altogether unpleasant. The merry chase was such fun and diversion. The thought of getting caught brought back her rosy glow, it was exciting and lots of fun. Not a bad way for an old lady to find out that men were still attracted to her…her proper Bostonian upbringing was ancient history!

Months passed and her quest for a great fantasy came back stronger than ever. To fly ! To be the solo pilot of an airplane! It is never too late to pick up old dreams and start again and set long-standing goals. With her usual determination she signed up for flying lessons, much to the horror of her retirement colleagues. Now or never was her mantra! She finally got her license to fly. Wings were pinned on her lapel amidst cheers, balloons and loud applause. She took over the controls of a single engine plane and soared into the blue yonder. She could not resist the temptation of doing a couple of loops over the roof of her retirement community and everyone screamed with delight! What an exhilarating time! No words can describe it. Her family was astounded but not surprised as they looked on and saw their little "girl" take off again. The shiny aircraft sparkled and disappeared into a puffy cloud never returning…

The melancholy suitors were unable to chase their beautiful princess. Their canes and walkers would not quite make the grade. Still undaunted and unworried, they happily waited for the day when they met again way up in the great beyond and yes, oh yes....their joyous pursuit would be resumed...for ever!

Draw Your Own Blueprints!

She was a sophisticated, highly educated and attractive woman, defying all description. Men stumbled just to have second look at her. Hollywood would have hired her in a heartbeat had she chosen stardom, but that was not part of her long range plan for life. She was the perfect "career woman", an architect by profession, yet back in the days when men ruled the roost and women were domestics confined to their houses, enslaved by pregnancies, cleaning, washing, cooking and exchanging recipes with other unsalaried laborers benevolently referred to as housewives. For amusement they took up group quilting and idle chatter. Husbands, on the other hand, often had supplementary activities outside their homes—so called affairs of the "heart", to avoid mentioning other parts of the male anatomy. They blamed their wives for frostiness in their own bedrooms. The comedy of errors started here. Such were the standards of that era, but not for this wife. She meticulously created her own bill of rights, holding firm to an unrevealed independence, all the while adhering to the regulations of those times.

Even though she had five children, her future was carefully tucked away out of sight for the day when freedom bells rang. Armed with vision and education, she was certain the moment would arrive sooner or later. As it often does, life changed direction, and her moment came sooner than expected. Quite a shock for everybody, her husband passed away suddenly. A life of stress, alcohol abuse, gambling, and extramarital affairs led to his abrupt demise.

His death brought sorrow to the family but a justifiable relief for his wife of many years. The independence she had fantasized about now came through the door with a big bang. As a capable architect, her "blue prints for life" had been secretly drawn and ready to be put to use when the right time came. This was it! A new day dawned fresh and ready for action!

Of all the widows interviewed, this one was indisputably relieved, not bereaved, admitting it openly. With the children now adults on their own, she was free to explore the bigger world that surrounded her. Off she went through the Americas first, then Europe. Emancipated beyond her expectations and enjoying every minute of it, she roamed the globe in awe and delight, viewing famous architectural treasures such as castles in Britain, the Eiffel Tower, Pyramids of Egypt, the statue of Christ atop a mountain overlooking the magnificent city of Rio, the Golden Gate Bridge in San Francisco, the tall buildings in New York, and many other architectural marvels of this magical planet. What a glorious time she had!

This brilliant career that had been waiting around the bend for along time was now about to sparkle. She moved to her native land of California, where the sky was her only limit. Her spirit had no boundaries! As an architect, she designed a variety of structures, each more beautiful than the other. Fame and fortune came pouring in easily, and a city avenue was named in her honor. Becoming successful and wealthy, she was looked upon by her old peers with admiration, disbelief, and a certain degree of envy as they wept over their knitting and home-made jams, dreaming of the day when they might achieve the opportunity to express themselves and wondering if it would ever really happen.

Now, to back up a bit about this world traveler's married life—not really recommended for the "how-to-tie-the-knot-and-live-happily-ever-after" manuals. Her husband resented her education and stylishness. Getting her pregnant five times was his form of reprisal, although it didn't slow down her ambitions. He often drank too much and assailed her with a barrage of abusive words for no reason other than the alcohol taking over. In the first few years of their marriage she had hopes that his behavior would subside; on the contrary, it increased along with the drinking. This was extremely upsetting to her, but after a while the predictable frequency of those eruptions caused her to go numb. Sensing their oncoming, she would don her emotional armor, letting his name-calling cruelty hit then bounce back. This was the only solution.

She was married very young, in her early twenties during the days when marriage was considered a "right of passage". If a young woman was not approached by a man before thirty years old, she was then destined to live the rest of her days as a solitary spinster with no visible means of support and facing a dreadfully bleak future—going to weddings, never catching the bouquets, leaving the parties in tears.

Time has changed, and the equality of the sexes has arrived. No longer do men kneel in front of lady, little velvet boxes in hand, asking them to be their wives, nor do they ask the lady's father to give her away as though she were property to be passed around. That custom was a condition of days gone by, predating dishwashers and microwave ovens…even The Joy of Cooking has lost its cheer. The inconveniences of that era are no longer trendy. Living is paradoxically both more complicated but also easier now. Who said we cannot have everything? Somebody was right!

Many widows when asked about their initial feelings regarding the death of their husbands responded sometimes with reticence or other times openly that they felt liberated to do what they chose with their lives, and not be defined by being the other half of a couple.

What advice would this particular widow pass on to others who lost their mates? Why didn't she remarry? She had plenty of chances. When I asked her this question she answered without a moment's hesitation: "There are so many mistakes to be made in one's lifetime, why make any of them more than once?"

Biblically Incorrect

One being was living perfectly content in Paradise Heights when the other was created. In this case who was there first? Eve of course! She really didn't need or pray for a help-mate but as it often happens, things appear, even people. One day a handsome guy came into view out of nowhere, calling himself Adam. Quite a glorious physique—"washboard abs", slightly tanned all over, tall, trim. He had the face of a Greek God, with flowing blond hair. But he was a miserable dresser, actually a no-dresser, wearing nothing but his Designer skin. Shocked and surprised, Eve complained to a higher authority, and the next day Adam was magically sporting the latest leaf of the season. She immediately thought about how that leaf would dry up later in the year—in the autumn when leaves do fall off—but decided that worrying too far ahead would not do. She went down town to the Eden-Falls Mall for a little shopping. Unwilling to give up her rib, she ended up paying an arm and a leg for fashionable outfits for this Adam who really didn't want any new clothes at all; he was comfortable with his leaf, happy with a great body. Why give up his favorite leaf right out of the garden? As often happens, the woman is more practical, while the man lives by his impulses. This is an ongoing dilemma.

After a few months in Paradise Heights and following the well-known apple skirmish, Eve made up her mind that they needed to relocate to a larger city where opportunities were more easily available and where no reptiles roamed freely, urging people to taste apples. Life had to be turned around for the better. They hopped a plane to Massachusetts where Adam went to Harvard and got his PhD in plant pathology. Once he graduated, he traveled to Central and South America specializing in the prevention of damage to tropical fruits and plants by insects, pesticides, or other harmful sources.

Adam and Eve didn't have a great deal in common, however. Contrasting backgrounds, different religions, values, families with dissimilar lifestyles and economic levels were increasingly apparent. Yet, opposites do attract, even if they bring on squabbles later. Eventually on one of his home leave visits, they were reacquainted, fell in love, and married. The wedding was elegant with chapel, reception, ring, flowers, music, dancing, champagne, multi-layered cake topped with the typical figure of newlyweds, the groom wearing a candy tuxedo. (Clothes on Adam! How sweet!) A long way from the old days of Paradise Heights, he had miraculously turned over a new leaf. Everyone was surprised and delighted with this transformation. Relatives remembered him from his unclothed younger days. How a strong woman can convert a man! Miracles do happen, timing is everything.

Their honeymoon was spent in Seventh Heaven Island. They had a marvelous time, even though Adam was still gazing tenderly at various leaves which reminded him of his bachelor days. A few years passed and they became parents of two appealing children, twin boys, Alfred and Cayne.

One day they had their first argument. Boom! Eve was a Zionist with dreams of going to Israel and working for the freedom movement. Her parents escaped from the Holocaust when she was a little girl, and she remembered deep suffering all around. What saved them was that her father, a medical doctor, was able to treat ailing prisoners and guards. It was through that path and at the right moment that he and his family fled their captors. Eve grew up aspiring to be a pioneer and help Jewish people gain their liberation. Adam thought the Israelis made monumental mistakes and would not stand a chance against the Palestinians. Two opposing views, but Eve was stalwart and intended to pursue her commitment to the cause, sooner or later.

She came from an upper middle class family, born in Austria, brought up and educated in Ecuador, lived in Costa Rica. He was from a modest New England family from Rhode Island, a seriously ambitious scholarly fellow, who was accepted at Harvard and graduated with honors.

They had busy and interesting lives, lots of travel and adjusting to customs in other countries and working well with people of assorted cultures. Adam was a dedicated plant pathologist, who authored several books on the subject. Eve, besides being a wonderful wife and mother, occupied herself with the advancement of peoples in the third world. Her dreams of returning to Israel never quite left her heart and mind, as she was hopeful that some day she would reach that goal.

Happily ever after lasted, but not for long. Adam contracted Parkinson's disease. This individual, respected and adored by Eve, the most incredible person she had ever known, was now unable to lead a normal life. How heartbreaking to see him incapable of continuing his long and noble career! Unable to eat, breathe, talk, move, he passed away the day of Eve's birthday, leaving her in complete distress and yet with relief to see his torture end. He had been a prisoner of his own body—in solitary confinement and unable to communicate with any one, not even by a slight final gesture. This left her depressed, angered, anguished yet at the same time relieved from her own suffering. A few days later, speaking at his funeral, she was able to put her feelings into words. His death on her birthday was like a gift to her—he gave her back her life!

Initially surrounded by friends and family, she had all the support she needed. However, as time went on, people who felt sorry for her and reminded her of the loss of her husband were more of a hindrance than help. After the funeral service, the family left, and she returned to her house. For the first time in her life she felt completely and silently alone. To this day she dislikes "the quiet". The minute she enters her apartment she turns on the TV, not to watch it but to fill the silence.

When as a married couple they had lived in Latin America, they had become involved in casual translations from Spanish to English and vice versa. Now as a widow, she decided to re-travel that path. Eventually she applied for an official position as an interpreter. After having to pass a difficult test along with many competitive applicants, she found success! Now she had her own career, defeating an obstacle and creating her dream. However, the thoughts of Israel never quite abandoned her heart and mind. Someday she would help with the liberation movement.

Several years later, when asked about her thoughts on

widowhood, she reflected that it was not the worse event that could happen unless the widow made it so. Grieving was acceptable, but not for ever. A couple of regrets were all right. If a career which had been started while married was neglected for reasons of husband and family, then it was best to pick up where it was left off and proceed from there. Do it in honor of his memory, and show the children that a wife/mother can go on solo. Or, just to be pleased and proud of oneself, do it for others.

Recently, a news article was written about a woman who traveled alone to Eastern Europe to help with negotiations between Israelites and the Palestinians. The article went on to describe a brave and determined young widow from a location called Paradise Heights. It left me wondering, could this be our Eve?

Bookends

She was invited to a dinner party, and there he was one of the many guests. Before they said the first word to each other her brain mulled over....what mellow elegance, refined low key manners and good looks...wouldn't mind getting to know him. Then they were introduced. What charm and magnetism to top all else. He was not a showoff, nor "high drama" similar to the previous partner who drove her out of her wits with frustration not to mention embarrassment. This divorcee was about to encounter a life mate who suited her immeasurably well and from this casual situation at a party a superior relationship was founded, the perfect union, the marriage not to be believed and yet genuine!

Not long afterwards, a few short years, he was stricken with a severe illness. Despite this turn of fate his playfulness and sense of humor never left him. She adored him and he blossomed under the magic spell of this attentive and loving wife. Although circumstances were threatening they grew happier each minute. Perfection is often fleeting and their time together was predestined to end not too far in the future. He had been infected with an incurable cancer, went through a series of treatments which left him weak, unable to continue his zesty way of living. To everyone's astonishment he never lost his lightheartedness and bewilderment and wonder at the most trivial aspects of life so many of us take for granted.

On one of the welcomed interrupted segments between chemo therapies his greatest desire was to go to a shopping mall at Christmas time. As they went through it, his eyes beamed like a child's, anticipating a visit with Santa Claus. He was filled with awe as they paused in front of one window then another. Every little thing was a source of joy and amusement. Had he had the strength he would have jumped up and down with the exhilaration of being alive experiencing the delights of the holiday season. He wanted an ice cream cone with chocolate sparkles on top. Not too long before while in the hospital, on a break from heavy medication he made a list of "fun things to do after chemo". Seeing a Christmas tree with all the lights on was part of this inventory. His wish now came true, a grown man aware that death was nearby, and yet capable of experiencing complete pleasure in the most minute moments of what was left of his time on earth. He wanted to sit by the river and see boats sail by, he asked for a trip to the zoo so he could watch the animals, he wanted to stare at the clouds and looked forward to snow so he could do angel wings on it…It was as though before departing the world for ever he wanted to return to his earliest childish self to complete the cycle of his journey.

This widow was simultaneously bereaved and yet relieved struggling with opposing feelings too difficult to put into words. She was thankful when the final hour arrived, the end of his torment, the beginning of her profound heartbreak. The most difficult moment of her life. How could anyone have loved him more deeply than she? Now when she gazes at surroundings they become inspiring and distressing all at once. Tears flow again thinking about how he would have appreciated that moment, sensing that he is somewhere, anywhere, energetic, his ever magnetic self spreading joy to those around him…an inward smile invades her thoughts. How she misses him and how spellbinding it is to realize that his presence is real, but not of this world.

Her reminiscence of the divorce years before was painful and filled with rancor. The memories of the marriage were sweet and loving. Unlike other cases widowhood for her was much more excruciating than divorce. Her thoughts. What helped? Counseling, not in a group but private. She researched and found the best there was. A close friend is always wonderful to have, someone who will cry, hug and laugh with you, talk about memories of the past and dreams of the future. Someone who never questions, just lets you ramble on and on. Someone who listens and never judges regardless of what you say.

This widow occasionally slipped into emotional "dark holes". Her friend let her jump in but lent her a hand when she wanted to come out into the bright light again. Never a word of criticism, no advice, no suggestions, only support and a caring heart.

Onward with reflections. Don't make any major decisions in the midst of grief, wait. It may be tough but let some time pass. What did not help? Official paper work, forms, attorneys, having to "think legal" when your mind is so far from such things. The costs are prohibitive and you're dealing with them because of a painful loss. Nothing is clear, including the vocabulary on documents, deeds, trusts and the like. Get someone to lend a hand besides a shoulder. More help. Get yourself healthy mentally and physically. Her counselor suggested that she write a letter to herself talking about regrets, uncomfortable moments, plans that might continue even without him, perhaps in his memory. An arrangement of life from then on.

Would she consider remarriage? Another robust negative! Nothing could ever replace the flawless companion. They were so perfect for each other they metaphorically resembled two book ends, capable of standing alone but holding so much more together from A to Z. Bereaved? Yes, but looking forward to unfamiliar possibilities.

Caramel

When two people have the same career in mind coupled with talent and perseverance, it is likely that they will eventually meet. This duo did, at New York University not quite by chance...which is the only way anything happens. Divine intervention maps out your life and you just follow the signs, being watchful not to get confused in the maze of choices. Not only were their academic interests a magnet for each other but personal chemistry added to the attraction. The legendary Cupid cooperates at times and destiny takes over before anyone even notices. Some call it magic, some call it love, others have another designation for it: life's mysterious movements! It happens a lot. Great poets have devoted their genius to describing this condition, and no one has ever been able to really figure out exactly what makes people drawn to each other.

He was bright, had a keen sense of humor, a princely physique and looked on her as a gift that dropped out of the out the sky in front of him. He went for her hook, line, and whatever else goes with this old quote. To add to this dream he was the dream fantasy of any Jewish girl—that is, he was a Jewish boy! What could possibly go wrong? Too good to be true and yet happening right there. From the minute they met it was violins playing soft music to which the lyrics said "Go on, go on you are meant for each other". His first Valentine's Day gift to her was a precious little kitten that purred when it wanted to be cuddled. She named it "Caramel" because of its color and sweet disposition.

These two students were instantly fascinated with each other, never even glanced or noticed another human being anywhere. They were inseparable, the veritable book ends that held up the wisdom of life together for ever. Before sinking half of his savings into the purchase of an engagement ring, he asked her father for approval to marry the only daughter. An exciting moment, as though he needed more electrifying times. It took some courage and shaky knees to face the old patriarch. The major criteria required were: Upstanding young Jewish fellow, who attended the synagogue regularly and faithfully, observed all Jewish Holy Days, plus all the other good traits required by a loving father to "give away" his only little princess. One key question from his side of the family, was she also Jewish? After hearing an enthusiastic "yes", the blessings and approval followed. From then on it was a piece of cake—wedding cake, that is! The big day arrived shortly after graduation. What a party that was! Lots of music, dancing, flowers, everything according to their religious traditions, families on both sides filled the synagogue and ball room.

This happy occasion was followed by the blissful ever-after of two people overwhelmingly taken with each other. They were two physical therapists who graduated at the same time and were destined to be together for life, an unbeatable combination. Any kinks or knots that might come would be solved without charge right in their own living room. Free therapy, seldom happens, what a deal! Two dazzling children were born to them. Unfortunately, the youngest one, while still a toddler, was found to have a speech disability which brought them much anxiety and years of expensive specialists to treat the child's difficulty. With a great deal of effort, sleepless nights and lots of expense this child was cured and went on to graduate from a major college in New England. The older offspring, a daughter, had a career and never married, dedicating herself to work and always very close to the family, especially her "baby brother".

For almost forty-six years this family experienced with delightful times and of course difficult ones as well. They had their share of struggles, fights, and merriments until one frightful day when the husband took his last breath in a hospice after being ill for an extended period. Up until the last few months he never really stopped or even slowed down his usual life style. He lived in the land of optimism and denial and hoped that somehow his illness would go away. Before he knew it death came into view, but with a kind approach. He had no pain and could maintain his jovial attitude till the very final moment. One minute alive, one minute gone…for ever. An earth-shattering event for the entire family. Silent disbelief and shock lingered for a time, especially for the wife. The ebullient husband, father, friend, lover, confidant, ever present was now absent. A difficult transition for a closely knit household unit. The widow now with grown children away from home had to go on with living unaccompanied. Paradoxically, to alleviate her grief, she would try to remember the times when he was so sick and would occasionally slip out of his perennially good disposition. In fact, for the previous few years he had not been quite himself, although he tried his best to conceal it. This mental approach of hers didn't help all that much; it alleviated her heartache somewhat but didn't really lead to total tranquility.

Little "Caramel", the purring darling of the family, had long been gone, and so her nights were even quieter. Caramel was a male cat and didn't produce a litter of candy colored kittens, much to everyone disappointment.

Before her husband had died, she had been grieving for a long time without anyone being aware of it. He had not been the same man she married all those years before…the energetic, buoyant person who loved the world and got such a kick out of life, had gone away for all time. Now, there was relief in that she was at last able to show her sorrow.

Remembering that he was not perfect (nor was she) also helped. They had different likes. Although they deeply enjoyed each other's company, they didn't do everything together. He never went to the theater with her, for example. She hated football games and attending one would be torture; seeing one on TV was a close second to "live" agony.

Soon after the grief became an integral part of the everyday, the family gradually acclimated to it, and life began to settle into its usual rhythm. There was no other choice. Not much changed. She continued doing the things she enjoyed this time with friends, or alone. The children were helpful but their young lives had to move forward towards a bright future awaiting them. She could not hold them back.

Grief groups were not the answer. She proceeded to create a life for herself, recalling the days when she was single and free to exercise her own options. It was easy and gratifying to slide into the old avenues again.

Would she consider re-marrying? A robust "no" was the reply. Her reasons not made clear, followed by a puzzling quiet.

Her advice for widows: "Get your finances in order even if you need to hire an advisor. It doesn't hurt to know how to manage your money in case you didn't do it before (as so often happened to women of her generation). Get busy. Start something. Be a detective, find yourself in case you had gone adrift in the sea of marriage, children and other related responsibilities. Her final words were of a softer nature: "Go to a shelter and adopt a purring kitten in need of attention. They make such sweet company. Their furry little ears are always alert and listen to you, ever agreeing with just one request: "cuddle me for hours and hours, please!" Meow…

Dynamite

    A gorgeous young man sat in front of her in class. As she looked at the back of his big large head covered with a mass of blond curls, she wondered if that head held together a good brain too. Brain and looks, that was more than one person deserved, she mused. He was always asking, debating, questioning the why's and how's of theories, driving the teachers either crazy or maybe to fantasize about another career.

    She was one of those who had a weakness for mind-over-muscle, despite being a cheerleader for the football team. She didn't admire the intellect of the players. They ran very fast on the field but indoors they sprinted away from the books more quickly than they chased the ball on the gridiron.

    Back to the fellow: he was a superior example of young humanity. She found out through the school's gossips that besides wits and unrelenting thirst for knowledge he was also a great dancer. What a combination, talented from head to toe! She made up her mind to attract him one way or another. Of course she would devise the perfect plot. Nothing really turned up instantly, and he went on ignoring her, unaware of her deep crush on him.

Graduation time arrived and the students were off to various colleges. The bright ones were accepted at the leading institutions. They ended up in the same university. Was that coincidence or destiny playing games with their lives? Who knows?

After certain classes he would just "by chance" wait around and give her a ride back to the dorm. He was socially inhibited, never really asking her for a date or saying anything that might lead to future encounters. This little diversion went on for a while until one day she "took the bull by the horns" and asked him out. This time the plan would work, she would capture him for certain. He was the offspring of a domineering mother and grew up skittish about making a move towards a female and being rejected. She had to take the first step. Beneath that gigantic body resided an insecure little boy frightened of the opposite sex. On the other hand, she was raised by a submissive mother and a tyrannical father. She remembers from childhood not liking that state of affairs and vowed never to follow in her mother's foot steps and be ordered about like a little obedient lamb around the house.

From then on it was down hill and sunny. They started going out every week end. He mellowed to the point of calling her. Their friendship progressed smoothly until the day she once again made up her mind. They were headed for marriage whether he knew it or not. Next, she proposed! He accepted more readily than she had ever dreamed he would. She dragged him to a store pointing out the diamond ring of her delight. No discussion. That was that! They were now engaged. The big blond puppy agreed to everything. A few months later they had a beautiful wedding enchanting both families. End of story? Not quite.

The marriage was reasonable for several years. However,

"reasonable" is not a thrilling description of any relationship. It tends to convey tolerable and that's what it was, just that…acceptable.

His intelligence, analytical capabilities and brain muscle propelled him into local government followed by national responsibilities. He blossomed as a statesman and a powerful politician, transforming his personality from submissive to authoritarian. He was now head of the household, dictating all the rules. The entire family was under his command and orders were issued and followed to the last detail, or else!

Life curved the other way and without warning, his wife slid into the submissive role disliking every minute of it. Was she becoming like her own mother accepting orders from a big dominant being? The once loving, kind, agreeable husband turned into a dreadful oppressor. Politics had gone to his head. His life had changed, and the giant persona was awakened in him. This could not continue forever she thought. There must be a way out. Meanwhile she began drinking to cover her alarm and distress. His associations with the "higher ups" in the capital, the dinners, cocktail parties, meetings, led him into overeating to mask his insecurities that still remained deep in his intimate feelings. She went along with this situation for the sake of the children and to maintain the appearance of a happy marriage, doing her best to prevent any potential scandal. Their life was not private. They were followed by media even when on vacations out of the country.

He was not unkind, a good provider, a good father to the kids although hardly ever at home to participate in their upbringing. She did it all and the drinking continued even though expertly disguised, no one noticed, not even the family. They lived in a huge country estate where they could entertain distinguished officials, ambassadors, legislators and their spouses almost every night. An exhausting schedule!

Food kept his hungry ego alive and well, and his eating got out of control as he tipped the scales at four hundred pounds. Doctors were consulted and discovered that he had an ailment that caused the veins towards the lungs to progressively shrink eventually leading to heart failure. He kept this hidden from his family for more than seven years, teasing his wife by saying that he was living much too long, robbing her of many long years of joyful widowhood. Meanwhile he silently prepared for the final day when his system would stop functioning.

She continued her charming ways and went along with the endless parties which were by now a way of life, the everlasting enchanting hostess making everyone feel welcomed and delighted to be there. Slowly she began to think of being emancipated from this excruciating situation. Often she contemplated divorce but the idea seemed too overwhelming at the time. Maybe with some effort this problem would resolve itself in the years to come.

The future arrived more promptly than expected. One day her husband announced that he had been ill for years with a lung disorder that would lead to a heart attack. He often had shortness of breath but attributed it to his weight and anxieties at work. He had been hiding it from family and friends not wanting to admit any weakness. This combined with back problems put him to bed for days. He blamed his corpulence for that as well. His arteries kept on closing in and the fatal day came into view suddenly and quietly. He died playing his own music, the marching band followed, flags, drums and all the rest! A majestic final act of a great leader. The "king" was dead.

At first she was shocked and angry at him for not confiding in her as though she would not take his side, comfort him or worse, possibly reject him. She thought back to the times when he jovially mentioned that he was "robbing her of her widowed life." Of course she was hurt but attributed these remarks to his frame of mind.

It was over now. End of an era, an arduous one. She needed a break and time to begin thinking of a future life for herself. A new chapter was about to be set in motion; the slate was clean. What to do now? What to do first? How to start? An idea! Sell the wretched country estate. Get rid of the monstrosity which was the source of many memories good and bad. Detaching herself from the past, she called a broker and in no time the place was sold, bringing in a sizeable profit. What next? She bought a penthouse condo overlooking her own domain, Central Park, New York. How enlivening to be in charge again! Her drinking stopped, no more entertaining every night, just when she felt like it, all the old habits were tossed out of her daily living, and everything started to hum—this time her own melody!

New home, new friends! In this environment she started a novel kind of companionship with a much younger man, a confirmed bachelor. They began to go out to theaters, dinners, dancing, sailing on cruises but never slept in the same bed. He was afraid of marriage, and so was she. A perfect combination, an enviable arrangement, it just did not get any better. There must be another name for widowhood, Autonomy, perhaps? Self-government?

Her reflections on widowhood: The major difficulty, especially when one is stressed, is paper work. Wills, trusts, deeds, certificates, insurance forms, all these had to be done lasting many weeks, a frustrating process. Another thing, being alone and not getting lonesome. Making all decisions on your own which are at first complex but get painless as time goes by. Living out life exactly as one pleases takes some adjustment.

She decided to honor his absence, conquering all her uncertainties and living merrily alone as an emancipated widow not married to someone in the often uncomfortable political setting. Their lives were never private, and the media of course was always around the corner ready and waiting to leap at the slightest sign of a potential scandal.

Would she consider remarrying? By no means, never! Once is enough. During their more strenuous moments she considered going to a marriage counselor but her husband would not hear of it. Admitting to any failure no matter how small, would be total humiliation, especially if the therapist turned out to be a woman. Never!

Advice to new widows: Find yourselves, be an example for your children, show them that life can be satisfying with or without a mate.It's not Noah's Ark, we don't always have to go in two by two…

The Galaxy Is Yours

Nine decades did not diminish her enthusiasm for life, her energy, sparkle, joy to be alive carrying such mountain of experience and knowledge! She felt as though she knew more than anyone else in the world and had to control herself not to talk "too big" and be a terminally boring little old lady.

Her blue eyes twinkled, her cheeks were rosy and glowing, plus the smile of someone in love as she was, with life! Always dressed in the latest fashion, "glammed up" to the hilt, her hair tussled with streaks of red, gray and blonde here and there, she could well qualify for the cover of any beauty magazine. The envy of the retirement community. Much to her delight she was the prime subject of the insecure gossipy types, pleased to supply them with something to talk about.

The day of the interview she opened the door and threw her arms around me with the world's most welcoming hug. I instantly felt as though we were dear old friends meeting again after a long absence and yet we had met the week before.

This interview showed great promise. It was filled with gusto and warmth. She exuded happiness. Later on during our talk I found out that her life had not always been perfect, on the contrary, often intimidating and distressing but her sense of lightness, faith, hope and good humor carried her through many a difficult spot. She did not allow bad times to influence her forever, just temporary blues now and again, her inner strength nudging her out of them when needed. She was determined not to let past sorrow grow into future grief. She knew intuitively that her life would level off returning with a good measure of joy. Was she ever right! Remember her mountain of knowledge and experience? Well she climbed over that peak many times but afterwards it was down hill and sunny all the way.

This vivacious lady was one of ten children. When I displayed surprise and amazement over this, she quickly giggled and said: "My mother didn't know what caused pregnancy". I giggled back and changed the subject before she told me all the details.

One of her talents was handling difficult situations; rescuing someone in distress, in this case her sister who was in a tottering marriage. Her hope was to coax the two of them back into a Romeo/Juliet type of relationship. No luck there. Her romantic visions for them quickly sunk into the sea of gloomy separation followed by a final divorce. Disappointed, broken hearted but with undaunted spirit she and her sister began to place their hearts and minds on what to do next. What now? Sustaining each other through this hurdle, they decided to start looking for employment and a place to live. They scoured the newspapers for work and shelter. One day they read about a boarding house with a vacancy for two sharing a room. Not far from it a down town restaurant where they were hired as waitresses. Life was shaping up again!

Trouble free and modest in their routine, the two sisters

energetically carried trays of food and cleared tables, cheerfully accepting gratuities to enhance their pay checks. Delighted patrons were willing to come back for such excellent service and tipped generously.

Their job went on for several months with nothing of any significance happening. Off to the restaurant and back to the boarding house was their daily humdrum routine, until one day when exciting developments started to bubble.

History quivered a little when one of the male guests of the boarding house forewarned his friend saying" Hey buddy, you better snag up the cute trick with the sparkly blue eyes or someone else will take her away before you know it". Right there and then this fellow decided he would heed his pal's advice and began a pleasurable heart throbbing chase! What fun, good for the circulation, his blood was running hot and cold at the same time, his heart was having the workout of its life! She was not looking for a man and not easy to catch, but the guy was unrelenting in his pursuit. They became friends and that's all she was really wanted. This camaraderie flowed on and special thoughts about the charming lad were slowly taking up space in her head…until the day when he knelt in front of her, gently held her hand, looked lovingly into her eyes which were by now starting to melt and while clutching a little velvet box between their hands asked her to be his wife. She, feigning a little surprise, whispered a breathless yes. She had really fallen in love with this guy from the start but would not admit it even to herself.

The wedding was a glorious, festive occasion. The town's cathedral overflowed with family, friends, acquaintances, restaurant patrons and the entire population of the old boarding house. They all came to wish them eternal happiness amid smiles and tears of joy. When the couple said "I do" and kissed, the congregation stood up cheered and applauded. A sumptuous buffet followed for the enjoyment of over one hundred guests.

They lived happily together for over fifty-two years. The day came when the couple's contentment was suddenly disrupted. The husband became very ill and in a few months was off to another life, leaving his happy world and a devoted wife who had stood by him at all times. When the final moment arrived, she was tenderly relieved to see him stop suffering at last. She wanted the best for him and at that point rest from pain was what he needed most.

This exuberant woman was left alone and heart broken. Her life would now change completely. The many years of total understanding and consideration they had for each other was no longer part of her days. They were inseparable companions. The times filled with enchantment and joy were a soothing memory for the rest of her life. Unfortunately they had no children; she would have to rely on the many long time devoted friends for support.

Her ever present faith and zest for life came to her rescue once more. It was time to center her attention on herself and go forward with the solitary though not hopeless future. She resumed her career of helping where there was a need and in doing so, her living took a turn for the better. She now resides in a retirement community and is still a source of contagious joy for everyone around her.

Her current big dream is of attending a star lit banquet in Heaven, escorted by a certain handsome friend she once met at a boarding house back on earth many years before they fell in love and married. She is positive that sooner or later there will be a special party "up there" and what an event that will be! Many friends, great food, beautiful music, even some of the past residents of the old boarding house, a reunion to delight all guests. They all knew one another way back when they had to look up at the sky to see the stars and the moon. Now they just have to glance down a little to see the whole universe, what a majestic view!

The trip of a lifetime was really worth it!

Is Happiness East of Here?

Would castles in the air become a reality overlooking the majestic snow covered Rockies? Would the Promised Land be East of California? For this young, effervescent, exquisite widow the answers were yes, maybe and no. Some of her dreams materialized, and some turned into nightmares. All she felt was the impulse to go away. Her adventuresome spirit propelled her into trying a life far from the Pacific Coast, a place she had loved for many years. But now for some inexplicable reason a force was sending her in another direction. Go East, whispered the wind. She yearned for the mountains, the pure air, the daunting peaks topped with snow staring at her as though they could read her thoughts. The sunsets out West were dazzling, although they brought with them a sense of melancholy that implored her to leave. Change of scenery had to be the answer. She left early on a crisp morning before the sun came up. Destination Denver, her adopted future home. The perfect spot on earth she envisaged.

Kismet followed her. Shortly after arriving there, excellent job offers appeared almost right away. She accepted the best one, of course. Exciting work though required attendance at long, tedious meetings. During those times her thoughts roamed around the conference table wondering why others might be doing the same. Were they there for similar reasons, looking for change, chasing rainbows or just getting ahead in the business world? One day in the midst of the usual meander her mind stopped on a fellow worker she had never noticed before. A handsome, intriguing type of guy, looking like "Super Man" minus a cape and mask. From his self assured manner he struck her as having an ego bigger than life, impressed with his own knowledge. What a snob, she thought. Her second notion was that he showed potential of being one enormous bore. She was wrong on all counts. He turned out to be an accomplished individual, knew his field well and was willing to share his expertise with others. Several meetings later it occurred to her that it might be wise to pay a little more attention to his skillful observations and gain knowledge from his excellent contributions.

In time she discovered him to be a kind, thoughtful person, not at all what she had imagined in the beginning. He was quite interested in the welfare of the community and did much towards the improvement of lives all around him. She could not help but feel great admiration for him. Little by little they developed a friendship for each other through common interests and a physical attraction began to gradually flourish between them. They dated occasionally and not long afterwards discovered that this casual connection had taken on a meaningful course. They simply had to be together all the time, a condition universally known as falling in love. Obviously the next step was a stroll down the aisle. Marriage! Yes!

One evening while out to dinner at a quaint mountainside chalet, he ordered a special champagne. The band played their favorite song, and he surprised her by dropping a sapphire ring into her glass as he proposed. An unforgettably romantic moment for both! The wedding took place some weeks later. They were happily together for over 18 years and had two endearing children who brought them much pride and delight.

Unexpectedly out of nowhere lightning struck. He was diagnosed with a brain tumor and given limited time to live. From then on turmoil ruled their lives. Doctor's appointments, chemo therapy, radiation treatments and numerous medications. They somehow muddled through that state of terrible anticipation until the dreaded day arrived. The prognosis had been three months, down hill all the way. The physicians had warned her that he might turn difficult, even unpleasant as a side effect of all the drugs but despite these warnings he remained his usual, loving, tender charming fellow that he had always been up to the last breath of life. When he died his whole family was left completely devastated in a state of insurmountable grief.

The burden was heavy. His loyalty, caring ways, good humor, joyfulness, all these sparkling qualities were suddenly not there. They simply had to go on with life cherishing and sharing the memories of this extraordinary father and loving husband. The mourning wife was not afraid of being alone, just heartbroken without the love of her life, the father of her precious children. The compassionate, understanding, companion her "other" self. Weeping came all time and clear thinking was impossible. They had shared all the tasks of raising their babies, dividing all the responsibilities of running the household. They were the model of the luckiest family on earth. Now emptiness permeated their every moment.

A counselor was consulted, it didn't help. Then therapist suggested aerobic exercises to bring up her endorphins possibly returning her sense of well being.

That didn't work. Nothing was of any use. Another doctor declared that her self esteem was at its lowest, and her situation beyond grasp. Time was the only cure.

Her husband was her happiness; he was her whole subsistence, an irreplaceable presence in her life. She could not live without him. This situation settled into a dark corner of her being with no hopefulness in sight. No clarity seemed to appear in the horizon. She felt alone, abandoned, out of the stream with other couples. Evenings were long and gloomy. Some people thought she might be desperate, disheartened, at a loss for any direction, as indeed she was. Others expected her to return to her busy productive career regaining her ebullient self; they were wrong. She couldn't. She was miserable. Her life became a series of disoriented tearful days, and these struggles were a constant reminder of her happy past. Her mind was a continuous cycle of turbulences facing the normal daily responsibilities at work and at home. Although she tried to get professional help everywhere, no one offered an iota of light regarding her situation. She felt demolished with sadness. The one person she trusted for so many years was gone for ever. Nothing would bring him back, not even the children, who were also grieving in their own way, could boost her towards any form of contentment.

Subsequently, after many sessions with psychiatrists, she began to show a more positive outlook and believe that someone else could possibly come into her life again…never to replace the one true love she had but to share the continuation of her days…

Reflections on widowhood? She quoted Louisa May Alcott…"love is the only thing we carry with us when we go, and it makes the end so easy"…Not for the ones who stayed…was her final comment.

La Vie Est Breve

For the narrative of this charming but reticent widow, I had to unearth her story word for word, like removing weeds from a garden of multi-colored flowers so that the beauty of their blossoms could be seen and the world could enjoy their splendor. Her life was filled with hills and valleys, storms and calms. Yet in talking with her, it seemed as though her existence was perpetually tranquil. The serenity in her manner puzzled me, as though a secret was tightly wrapped in a package, and I had to open it carefully to view the contents. My curiosity gradually evolved into the satisfaction of getting to know this enigmatic person and her interesting life.

Her husband was suddenly taken away in a car accident caused by a drunk driver. In one instant she was alone, a woman in the peak of her life with three children under nine years old. She and her husband had been together many years, blissful times, and in one atrocious moment, their lives were interrupted. In his case, death abruptly ended that life. An extremely painful moment, a sad finish. She was numb with shock and despair but knew she had to live for the sake of her offspring…managing her to veil her heartbreak for the benefit of the rest of the young family. Life stumbled forward day by day.

As we got acquainted, I noticed that one of her charms was her total lack of concern about enhancing her appearance. She had that take-me-or-leave-me outlook, and that if you choose to leave, please don't stir up too much dust. Unbeknownst to her, she had me captivated in jealous amazement at such a mellow approach to live. She was competent for giving lectures on peacefulness without requiring one to check into the nearest monastery, sleep on cold cement, sip herbal teas, or chant one's way into this "nirvana" of hers.

As for the possibility of remarriage, who knew, someday maybe, but she didn't lay awake at nights being consumed with the prospect of where or when that second Prince Charming would show up. However, fourteen years later through friends at a dinner party there he was in the flesh! The Prince! An instant connection. Butterflies danced in her stomach. What was really happening? Was she in the middle of a delicious dream?

Months went by and they were married. There were children from both sides, a blended family. He had been widowed and so brought to this marriage his two children. He was a few years younger than she was, but who is counting or cares? Happiness has been theirs to this day. She felt fortunate to find contentment again. He a personable, kind, energetic, health-conscious person, vigilant about the food his family ate. He even took his lunch to the office every day and rode his bicycle there several miles each way. He was a handsome, blue-eyed guy with tenderness in his glance…and possessed "joie de vivre" and enthusiasm that should have been allocated to more than one person. He had it all, and now they had each other. Life was idyllic…Some people inexplicably get everything. Go figure…

She and her husband plus merged brood were transferred to France. She was pregnant at the time. When people inquired about her having a baby in a foreign country her unruffled answer was, "Don't they have them there too?" As it turned out the baby was born in the United States before they set sail on the unpredictable North Atlantic waters heading towards the Old Continent.

France was new to them and so was its citizens' slight arrogance, implying that any attempt at belonging there was futile. They would always be Americans. Not speaking the language fluently was an immediate disadvantage. Not so with the kids. They assimilated well and quickly, mingled right in with their peers, and picked up French as effortlessly as children do. Shopping was another story. The French clerks were difficult to understand, and she often came home without the goods she intended to buy. When she finally mastered enough verbal skills to get by, life was much easier! After a year or two she was relieved to come back to the United States, leaving behind some casual French friends who never wrote other than the occasional Christmas card. They settled back to life at home in New York State, and later moved to Maryland, where they currently live.

An interesting digression worthy of note. This is a woman who married twice, was happy each time while few others experience the same joy in their lives, and more than once?! What great thinker conjured up the thought that life is not always fair? This philosopher may be gone by now, he did not live to see that oftentimes life is more than fair, it's downright fabulous! Theorists are not always good predictors of destiny, that's the problem.

This captivating woman was not the typical mother and

housewife. In fact, without driving a car, she systematically did all the errands, took kids to and from a variety of schools activities, shopped and carried out all the duties associated with running a smooth household…all this on public transportation. Admirable, isn't it? Complaints? None! Life had to go forward. Such was my bewilderment at her remarkable way of approaching life that I found myself driven into temporary silence.

As time slipped away, and her children grew up, she decided to pursue an old dream—to go to college. Her affinity for the arts and social work led her into pursuing a degree in those disciplines. Graduation was exceptionally thrilling for her, as she was the oldest student to receive a degree that year. A fantasy became a reality, once more with no clamor.

After all the adjustments she had made, raising several children, getting a college degree, what would follow all this? In her case no deafening explosions were heard. Time went on as usual, day in and day out, sunrises and sunsets…her serenity remained. She was by nature a person who could take all that came her way and not let it subjugate her emotions. She had a most astonishing personality, difficult to believe and yet so authentic. An extraordinary individual!

Reflections on widowhood: "Not something I would recommend", she calmly states. "It brings on isolation, I missed the companionship, the intimate moments, the co-parenting, the times of loving laughter".

Advice to other widows: "Choose a path and go with it. A support group is helpful. Keep your head, don't do anything impetuously. Life has a way of advancing so follow it, there is no other way. Decide to be happy, no one else will do it for you. Life is short, you see, "La vie est breve".

Love at Any Age

Young love, real or infatuation? Her desk was in front of his in the class room. They often helped each other with homework's difficulties. These were dilemmas in those days seemingly impossible to solve but undemanding, compared to what the future would bring later on in life. For these two blushing adolescents life was enjoyable and uncomplicated. On weekends they would go to the country club's swimming pool where he would proudly display his football muscles while she would dive in the water pretending to be a willowy mermaid. They were in love…who could describe it? It would take one hundred poets to write about it and as many artists to capture them on canvas. On Saturday nights they went to special dances, and the zeal for each other shimmered on the dance floor. After graduation they were accepted at different universities, following their parents' wishes that they attend their alma maters. A few years later they met again, only to rekindle their attraction for each other. Their feelings had not subsided.On the contrary, they were living proof of the maxim "absence does make the heart grow fonder". The spark was still there, brighter than ever. A few months passed, and he popped the proverbial question. She accepted—to the delight of both families who had been close friends for generations before. A wedding ceremony took place in the local chapel, lots of flowers, music, one hundred or so guests, a magnificently tiered cake with the memorable candied couple on top, tears and smiles all around, a festive occasion not to be forgotten for years to come. The happy couple boarded a luxury liner en route to what is known as the most romantic city in the world—Rio de Janeiro, Brazil. Seven days at sea, balmy weather, calm waters, sunny days, moonlit nights, a dream could not have been more enthralling!

From this radiant merger two children were born—babies who went from cuddly to handsome, smart, educated, successful dedicated and accomplished sons. A source of pride and joy for the entire clan.

Their mother, now a great grandmother, did not look at all her age. Slender, petite fashionably dressed, always poised and self confident. A cheery, loyal friend to all who knew her and a pleasure to have around. One of her qualities was serenity. She carried that quality around, passing it to others and creating an atmosphere of calm elegance wherever she went.

After thirty-eight years of a happy life together, her husband began to show consistent symptoms of weakness followed by heart problems. When the diagnosis was completed, it was discovered that the cause was the overuse of cigarettes. He was a constant smoker. He immediately quit, unfortunately too late. In the prime of his life his breath was taken away from him. Lung cancer took over. This lively, energetic, enthusiastic, humorous human being departed from this world on the eve of his sixty-fourth birthday.

Hiding behind her tranquil appearance, she was burdened with an overwhelming sadness and emptiness, a longing for her partner of so many years. She deeply missed him and yet from that moment on some obscure reason prevented her from breaking down with tears of sorrow at no longer having him as part of their lives.

Shortly after his death she too developed health problems. A malignant tumor was found but removed in time. After several weeks of therapy and rest, she regained her physical condition and could resume life's activities.

Simultaneously daze and grief took over and it seemed unachievable to recuperate from all those difficulties. Quite a long time went by before she arrived at the painful realization that she was now permanently alone. Several months went by before she gathered the strength to drive to her husband's office. That day, for the first time she allowed herself to weep and the tears cascaded down her cheeks uncontrollably. Her sobs were in a way restorative, helping her soothe profound emotions held for so long. That moment was her initial encounter with reality. She was now able to think clearly and start directing her fragmented heart towards a positive course and happiness once again.

When I asked her about her thoughts on marriage she responded with a twinkle of a smile… A sharing of ideals, a loving partner, an excitement at being in each other's company. What were her unaccompanied plans for the future? Nothing immediate, but considering her recent surgery she decided it was time to grasp a new lease in life and do something. She didn't quite know what, perhaps a fresh point of view…who knew what might crop up? Her spirit was unlocked to inner or outer suggestions, ready to engage in anything!

One day her heart spoke up! A bright idea knocked on her mind's door with a loud bang! All of a sudden she was certain. She knew! A support group for widows, a forum where they could comfortably share their feelings, give each other suggestions, talk about their feelings, deal with problems, find solutions, exchange viewpoints, openly weep and encourage each other, generally lending a hand as new situations arose. That was it! A mission to accomplish, a loving, purposeful one at that.

She then moved into a retirement community—the perfect place for her noble calling. The groups started out small. People were shy about communicating their grief to total strangers, but gradually as new ladies joined, the group began to expand in the warmest ways. Widows found out that they had much in common and formed other groups in the neighborhood. When the word got around to the press, she was asked to give lectures on the initiative, ending up on television interviews reaching large audiences. She became valuable and known to so many that she never had another lonely moment or a minute to spare with a full calendar of activities. Living was good, contentment had at last appeared. Of course she often thought about her wonderful husband and wondered if he could watch her from "on high". Wouldn't he be overjoyed and not at all surprised?

Her suggestion to other widows: In assisting others you also greatly help yourself. It is true indeed that in giving you receive more than you can possibly imagine or ever wish for in life. Living becomes useful once again.

She has recently died, taking with her memories of years well lived, a family, a loyal best friend a sweetheart. I have a strong sensation that they ultimately met again this time not in high school…way up beyond cloud nine!

The Rings Kept Their Promise

Dreams… Who doesn't have one or more? Many think their fantasy is too insignificant not worth mentioning. Some regard their visualization so wild it is safer not to make it known…so why bother? Large or small, untamed or trivial, if they are abandoned they will evaporate! Some people however, tackle their aspirations with such enthusiasm they reach the summit forgetting how arduous the climb was.

This is the narrative of a woman's vision, her story had to be told. Would legal action be brought against her if she revealed everything, complete with names? What format would she choose? Maybe a humorous one ? A lot can be told in jest. Her dream was strong and fragile at the same time. She was suspended in hesitation…what to do? One day it "hit" her. A creative and yet not far from reality account of her experiences involving people in her life. No identities exposed, prudent in anonymity. She was an entertaining, humorous person and people often suggested she'd try for stand-up comedy, although she preferred writing…longer lasting final product and a larger audience; fame and profit did not escape her reasoning. Who knows, maybe she might win a literary prize, the great award for witty narrative? She felt she was really on to something. Her idea was shaping up, becoming clearer as time went. Didn't someone say that "a genius is someone who aims and shoots at something nobody else sees and hits it" ? The title of her book now dawned on her…a flash of inspiration! "It Won't Be Boring". That's it, at last! Who in possession of a right mind would ever think that boring was enjoyable? This charming, energetic, attractive widow did not wish for a tedious mind numbing existence and she didn't get one!

The major part of her career as a social worker included interviewing people and helping them find employment. The candidates were placed according to their strengths and weaknesses. As she talked to them, she had to estimate their potential for occupations with respectable salaries and benefits. She didn't particularly enjoy this profession but the money was good and helped her maintain a comfortable life style.

One day a new interviewee appeared. Surprise of surprises! Not a pathetic, disadvantaged human being in need of assistance, rather a tanned, rugged, good-looking male, appearing to be in top-notch physical condition, although walking with a limp using a cane. Poetry in motion! It's not every day that we run into hobbling hunks. He apologized for being a bit late having just stepped out of his sail boat after returning from a trip around the North Atlantic. The whole scene was so startling it propelled her towards a major melt down. After catching her breath and returning to normal she mused…how astonishing, adventurous, romantic…and yet how not for her, really. Queasy thoughts swayed in her head at the thought of sails boats. Her only fantasies of the high seas revolved around big ocean liners, with large white chairs scattered on the decks, sportily dressed passengers loafing, sipping drinks, reading, chatting with each other or dozing away the hours. A staff of refined stewards in impeccably starched elegant uniforms moving around quietly catering to every person's desire. Any vessel the slightest bit smaller than these luxurious passenger ships would instantly represent an adventure of life threatening proportions.

The interview with this fellow was to take about one hour. It lasted six! The attraction was immediate and intuitive. She was not ready for this, having not long before escaped from an unfortunate experience with the opposite gender leaving her somewhat wiser and more careful about such matters…besides, it was not part of her job description to even consider "falling in love" with a client. That would not look favorable in her next resume, and the way things were going she might soon be in need of one.

In the cool light of the morning of the next she would reflect on this incident and return to her senses. In the absence of level-headed consideration plus a restless night, she found herself passionately "head over heels" with this person she had just met the day before. What an unexpected turn of events!

At times like these she hoped that good judgment would surface and take over the emotionally disabling feelings that reigned in her heart. After all they met just 24 hours before as she was merely trying to do an honest days' work. It appears that the shuffling hunk was another unwise individual who also fell madly in love with her. When they met again the world came to one of those moments when it stops going around normally and it begins whirling intensely. Being near him turned the skies blue, sea gulls squealed with joy, waves rolled, sails flapped in the wind and ocean currents swept them to new horizons. They were off! All this without leaving the shore was downright frightening!

These two people were an item for life! They were married after a few months. Engraved on the inside of each wedding band were the words: "it won't be boring"... He was a quick moving person in all aspects, part of his charisma cane and all. They were happy for years...monotonous moments? Never! The rings kept their promise.

One day all of this came to a sudden halt. He died in the prime of life. His death was followed by a great deal of sadness. Two daughters were inconsolable not to mention the wife who was completely overwhelmed by this appalling unexpected event. This young woman did not know what to do next. The grief was too much to bear. She had to console the girls when she needed a lot of support herself not quite sure which way to turn.

In an effort to discover some guidance she joined a widow's group but found no solace there. All they had in common was widowhood, not the same issues or expectations. She had to face life dealing with all the ensuing anxieties on her own. Everything started over, this time as a single mother of two broken-hearted teenagers. Friends tried to be helpful, inviting her to their functions in an effort to bring some joy to her but she had the daughters to consider. She began tackling projects with great fervor. Her day to day living began to revolve around the two girl's activities. Holidays were celebrated as though their Dad was still there. Though he was Jewish, his Christmas stocking hung on the fire place with great care and a place setting was arranged for him at the Thanksgiving table. To this day his words are in heard in the voice mail of their phone.

It was difficult to console the youngsters. They deeply felt both parents should be home when they left for college, not have one gone away so suddenly. Their immature spirits were confused, especially for the older one who was taken by her father to several universities for interviews and now had to make the final decision without him.

People who had never gone through the loss of one partner assumed that she had so much less to do than before, when in reality her duties now doubled. She became two parents embodied into one. Well meaning friends not understanding the situation suggested that she go into volunteer work to pass the time away as though her life was now filled with empty space. She was busier than ever with double duties in every direction. Tasks shared with her husband were now carried out alone. The weight of grief was heavy on her shoulders but she had to survive it, with no previous training. This was a marathon for the emotionally fittest with the final line seemingly moving away as she ran towards it. When she at last reached the finishing goal, exhaustion coupled with a sensation of accomplishment beyond description filled her being. That race that had to be run alone, there were no competitors.

They had a few house pets including a furry, benign, thoughtful dog with emotional issues but affectionate and harmless. Such a considerate old pup tried not to shed hairs on the carpet causing more work for the single master already laden with enough problems. This large lump of fur became known as the "guardian angel" ever faithful to the former owner having stayed by his side till the very end.

Reflections: She did not want to return to the work force right away or to volunteer just to be useful and pass the time. In her views these activities resembled care giving and supervising others brought parenting to her mind. What to do with widowhood? She read everything she could find on the subject of grief, single parenting, loneliness but the overwhelming feelings of sadness and loss prevailed. Each person has to handle these difficult times the best way possible. She had to deal with this alone. Emotionless, senseless paths, a variety of maneuvers, irrational turns here and there eventually led her to the arrival of tranquility, living under her own terms facing all the ups and down with courage.

Children's rebellions were a little more thorny than they would have been if their father were around sharing, supporting and disciplining. Good and bad days came and went. Everybody endured them to the best of their capabilities. Then one day life began to flow again smoothly, at times irregularly as lives go. There was only one captain of this boat now to be congratulated or blamed for what happened, depending on how calm or rough the waters were. It was lonely at the helm.

She tried the dating scene. It malfunctioned. The first attempt was Mr. Wonderful, blessed with no problems of self-admiration…indescribably tiresome. The next one claimed that he made women weep, unaware that their gloom was really due to his presence—grounds for any human being to go into long-term depression. The third one turned out to be widowed "grandpa" with rubberized sensible shoes, plaid flannel shirt, claiming to be fifty but with the appearance and demeanor of many more decades on this planet. The most unbearable thing about him was referring to his deceased wife as "pick of the litter". Her conclusion after these experiences: grateful to have attempted but happy getaway from this research.

Would she remarry? Yes, she quipped, depending on a multitude of factors worthy of some consideration. He would have to be someone extraordinarily special, in total harmony with her way of thinking. That was the most important prerequisite.

How about going at it alone? Well, she pondered, there are advantages and difficulties with any couple's lives. Who knows what the future has in store for any of us?

Her marriage had brought along many happy and some discontented times but one thing for absolutely sure there was never a boring moment. The rings indeed kept their promise!

Out of Her Shell

She had an interest in oceanography and natural history, and was an enthusiastic member of the Shell Club of America which was having its annual meeting in New York City the very day she arrived in town. The world's number one mollusk guru was the featured speaker for the afternoon. She simply could not miss it! What better chance would she ever have to hear and meet this formidable human being?

Life doesn't always rotate clockwise even north of the Equator. The famous expert would turn out to be her future husband. Who would have predicted that? Their meeting was purely accidental. Fascinated by each other's charms there was instant chemistry. She, immensely impressed by his grandeur and he, magnetized by her "femme fatale" energy. It so happens that at that time she was looking for a job. A twice divorced woman mother of three kids with no help from the various exes. Finances were tight, and she needed money to keep things going. He was looking for a secretary/personal assistant and offered her employment which she promptly accepted. What a dream come true for her! The ideal occupation plus wages. What a perfect fit…minds on the same theme, it just could not get any better. One caveat: she had to relocate to another state at a moment's notice, live next door to him and be accessible twenty four hours a day at the mercy of his sudden capricious inspirations. A type of slavery…

This arrangement went on for three years or so when he determined that she reached the criteria to be his third wife. He had been widowed twice before and the previous wives might have been somewhat glad to depart. He had been an egocentric, difficult, demanding husband, complicated by any evaluation. She had doubts at first, but decided to go ahead and accept this marriage proposal despite trepidations. Her hopes were that he would mellow, become more loving with age and they would find happiness together. She was wrong! He got progressively worse. This voyage was heading quickly into stormy waters. Living with him was a kind of torture although it magically lasted for twenty years. During the last five he contracted a terminal lung disorder that led him to his death. He had to live under an oxygen tent and one fateful night she found him lifeless in bed. He was gone.

He was world famous in the arena of crustaceans, had a huge following and authored over forty books on he subject. This nourished his profound need to be admired and adored by many. One wife did not satisfy his thirst for approbation. Fame was what he wanted above all and he guarded it with his life until the very end.

This marriage was turbulent and exciting at the same time. Trips around the world, special appearances as honored guests and "shell" reunions, parties, newspaper interviews and articles featuring them. There was never a moment when the two of them shared thoughts, exchanged hopes, dreams, fears or plans. They were not soul mates…just existed together. The anguish of loneliness reigned in her heart despite their unstable marriage.

Having been an independent woman, although not admitting it to him fearing insults in return, she now had a sense of gladness not having him around, living life in the single lane again making her own decisions. There was a lot of work in settling his estate. Writing notices to several publications all over the world, social registers, magazines and the media. He left a museum to be looked after and many books to be distributed to his heirs, a great estate to be put on order. Not an easy task but somehow sprinkled with a certain touch of quiet relief. The most intricate part of it all was partitioning off his mollusk library of world famous writings to the designated parties. Exhausting effort and yet each day brought on a twinge of finale as a reward. She quickly got accustomed to his absence, physical and emotional.

Once the holdings were settled and all the paper work completed, she began to give thought to life in the future tense. At this point her children were on their own. She truly was in an empty nest with only herself to consider. The voyage started all over again, the seas were now calm, the skies sunny, the sun shining and sails were flapping in the gentle breezes of destiny. Destination unknown.

A remarkable and yet depressing element of our interview was that she talked at length about everything except mourning or even some recollection of the few happy moments they had enjoyed together. During our discussions she acknowledged the joy of freedom from his tyrannical ways. There was an immense pleasure in not being dominated by a self absorbing mate.

Now for her goals. First on the list: stop drinking, a habit she acquired during the days of marriage to that imposing individual. Such was the nervous tension during their association that she turned to alcohol as a retreat from anxiety. She signed up for Alcoholics Anonymous and in a relatively short time got rid of the dreadful pattern. The second wish was to learn how to play the saxophone. While at AA she met someone who was a musician and together they shared their talents and ambitions. He turned out to be quite a good companion and they decided to join residences and become partners, not really marrying, just living with each other without the blessings of altar or paper work.

Life went on trouble free, not exciting just uneventfully serene…enormously different from the old days of conflict, turmoil, fights, drinking and emotional roller coasters. Nowadays, they walk on the beach every morning, grand children visit, holidays are celebrated, New Year's resolutions are made and broken, sunrises and sunsets enjoyed. Cups of coffee by the moonlight on cool nights, unending conversations…life goes on!

Happiness and serenity now reign, not a bad way to be, at last out of her shell…

The Silent Explosion

World War II was happening and bombs were being dropped day and night over London. A gloomy, terrifying time for the British.

One explosion however during a crisp misty morning never made noise or frightened the general population. It took place in the hearts of two people who just met quite by chance. He, an American pilot walked into the Headquarters of the British Foreign Office and she, a young woman working as a secretary, doing her best to help her country's war effort by busily striking at the typewriter's keys while praying that the war would end soon. The instant they greeted an immediate magnetism burst in their hearts and minds with the force of a thousand soundless bombs falling from the skies. If there been an air attack at that moment it would not have been heard or even noticed by those two. Fate marched in and transported them into another sphere, propelling their destinies to live life as one, for ever. A strong liaison was created that day.

Despite the age difference a bond formed between them, the attraction was overwhelming. He had been divorced before and had adult children. She was single and young. Regardless of barriers they discovered that they had a great deal in common and began to see each other frequently. Almost every evening they met for long fireside chats, sharing dreams, planning for a future together, had dinners, walks, theater, all sorts of enjoyable times getting more and more attached even in the midst of all the confusion. The war appeared to be far away and hushed when they were close to each other, holding hands. Inseparable was the best description for that pair. At the end of late evenings he would escort her through the blacked out London streets and kiss her goodnight by her garden gate, yet never to be invited in. She lived with her family and they were not aware of this alliance with the Yankee fellow. She had not told them, fearing their disapproval. Eventually they all had to meet. Her family was won over by this charming person almost immediately. They became very fond of him, except for one horrifying thought. Would he whisk her off to America? The family was closely knit, and the idea of their only daughter going to another country an ocean away was agonizing.

Weeks went by and their relationship grew stronger. When he proposed marriage to her, she flew into the air and joyfully accepted. A lovely wedding was carefully planned but for one impediment. The Church of England would not permit a previously divorced person to be married in their house of worship. The whole family was greatly disheartened, as they had been faithful parishioners for generations and had contributed much to the church's resources; but the priests stood firm to their set of laws. Awkwardly the young couple settled for a nearby chapel of another denomination and the wedding took place as planned. A beautiful ceremony with every member of the family present. The lovely small cathedral was filled with the aroma of flowers, amidst the tears and smiles of everyone. The bride and groom were radiant. Champagne and cake followed the service out in the parish gardens. The British weather cooperated by caressing them all with warm sunshine. A magical time was had by all.

What was in the forecast for these two? They were married for nearly thirty years and adopted two girls. The unwelcomed future arrived much too soon. The husband began having spells of depression, drinking and causing difficulties for all. He always apologized profusely between bouts of such terrible behavior, but his attacks started happening more frequently. The most perplexing times were when his temper flared up and he started mistreating and abusing the children. This situation was extremely upsetting to his wife who then slipped into a constant tension which led to chronic ailments. As time passed she became more and more melancholy and progressively under the weather. The husband's turmoil was a source of several disorders which caused him to end up getting a severe case of emphysema taking him to his death after much pain and suffering.

The wife entered into a state of shock, grief, anger and hushed relief. What to do next? She did not miss her husband's obnoxious behavior so damaging to everyone. There had been many years of torture and sleepless nights for herself, her daughters and of course, not one upsetting word to her family back in London.

Her burden was lifted, but replacing it was confusion. What to do next? She was facing a new life that in time changed into days of peaceful routine a sort of harmonious loneliness. The turbulent times were over, new horizons to conquer, rainbows to be chased, life was agreeable…good memories lingered on despite the bad moments.

She returned to the job outside the home to supplement the family's budget comfortably supporting herself and the children. Some years later the daughters became adults and left home to pursue their own lives. She found herself alone in charge of her own destiny to do whatever she pleased any time she desired. She now had to bear it all, emotionally and practically but after surviving the terrible past she had no difficulties with this new challenging future.

When asked if she considered remarriage her prompt answer was a quick "no more wedding bells for me, thank you"! She was quite at ease with her unaccompanied existence. During her travels throughout the world when hotel clerks inquired "how many in your party?", she responded with restrained delight, "Party of one, please".

Tale of Two Widows

When a woman lives way out in the country with just her husband and one day he suddenly dies…the result is untainted loneliness. Farm animals don't talk, argue, agree, discuss events with you or even chat on about farm gossip. A daily conversation with yourself in front of a mirror isn't considered rational. Eventually after a few solitary dialogues when you know the questions and the answers, the possibility of thinking yourself as bizarre strikes you. The thought of being ready to join others in the same condition safely locked up in a mental hospital dawns dangerously in the horizon. This distressed woman had good fortune on her side. Her charming, high-spirited niece began to visit her regularly, every week end.

Her niece, who was also widowed unexpectedly, was a day brightener for the elder one. She arrived laden with gifts, flowers and surprises bringing life to the place. The vast difference between the two was that the younger one was not bereaved, not even mildly depressed. Her marriage had been a disastrous one. Since the death of her husband, she became free of the immense burden she carried for years. He drank himself to death to put it briefly… She was an active divorce attorney in town and her demanding schedule only allowed her trips to the country on week ends. In her work she was entirely acquainted with unresolved marital problems that led men and women to separation for other than death and felt great empathy for those who spent large sums of money only to be disconnected legally from each other with one being left discarded. Her husband's abuse of alcohol was intolerable and many a night she had to pick him up off the floor and drag him to bed while he mumbled incoherently about life's miserable times. When he "kicked the bucket" his legacy to her was complete independence. Her life became serene and worries vanished. Evenings were spent doing as she pleased alone or with friends. He may have gone to alcoholic's heaven but she stayed earth bound in her own paradise of tranquility. Most widows don't wish to make this known, but in a shrouded way many admit it.

How did she meet him? Amusingly enough, at her auntie's house during one of her week end visits. He lived there in one of the rented rooms. The farmhouse had been gloomy and unexciting with the old lady echoing about, making her all the more aware of her wonderful husband's absence. Having a few people occupying the rooms did wonders for the atmosphere of the place. Noises all around, cups left in the kitchen sink, the faint aroma of after shave lotion, (she rented to men only), cell phones ringing off and on, all this made her feel safe as though her husband were still in a way at hand bringing energy to the old creaky mansion. Not to mention the extra income that added to her pension making life more comfortable. Nothing like a touch of testosterone to stir up the old homestead after all.

One night, as the niece sat with her aunt by the fire sipping sherry, down the stairs came a handsome, well dressed gentleman. He stopped as usual for a short chat and the two were introduced to each other. The magnetism was instant! You could almost see it in the air. She didn't meet him again for several weeks until one night as he came down the stairs once more, paused for a while longer than usual and they engaged in a fascinating conversation, leaving auntie fast asleep in her chair after listening to the two of them for hours. He wanted to know all about her, quaking at the fact that she was a divorce attorney specializing in expensive break ups between people and yet so charming and lovely. It was difficult to imagine a bundle of femininity in a such a harsh career. On one occasion he finally managed to invite her out to dinner at a local posh restaurant. She accepted. Afterwards they went dancing swirling around the floor as though they had been practicing for years. What a pair. They danced till dawn and then went back to where they were staying together. After all they slept in the same house…separate rooms, of course.

Time and time again they went out finding out more about each other and enjoying every moment of their new discoveries. One evening at dinner they were holding hands as the music seemed to soften and he slipped a ring on her finger while whispering. "Would you be my wife for ever and ever?" She was ecstatic, barely murmuring an ardent "Yes, of course!" She was intensely in love with him, and they kissed right there in front of everybody, a kiss that lasted longer than the civilized limits of public displays of affection. The other patrons of the club caught on and applauded. The band went played on with extra zest. The beginning of a new life for them. Ah, beginning, such a charming and hopeful word we forget that there is an ending to it all…

They were married for many years and had three sons. Their union was not always perfect. He drank quite a bit habitually but it increased considerably after their middle son committed suicide at only twenty two years of age, a bright but introspective young fellow with a promising future ahead. To add to the misfortune the local police temporarily suspected the father of shooting his own son. After some investigation it was established that it was indeed was suicide. No note was left adding to their sadness. Their boy was gone.

From then on the couple's relationship fell into greater strain. Soon after this terrible event, he began to go on drinking binges. One day he arrived home went up to his room to take a nap and simply never woke up. He breathed his last quietly and suddenly. No warning, no note. The end.

Her reflections on widowhood. She went back to the career she had abandoned while married and raising three boys. Her law firm took her back with open arms. She was a competent lawyer and unfortunately divorces were more rampant than ever before. Single again, a working mother of two sons in college she tackled life with gusto and earned a salary sufficient to continue the life style as before. Advice for new widows: "If you don't have a career, get one, go back to school, do what you've always wanted to do but had no time or energy left in previous years. Wake up and seize your dreams, now is the time".

Three Ships

Three trips to the altar? This story brings to mind Christopher Columbus negotiating with Queen Isabella to acquire three vessels and set sail on the unknown seas searching for "the new world". This widow was married three times looking for happiness on the other side of her rainbow. Columbus found America. She, after much charting and sailing through some rough waters found an island...herself! When it was all over she pondered had the effort been worth all the risks?. Of course, yes!

At this juncture of life in her early middle years, she felt confident enough to confront any event that might arise, acquiring along the way the insight on how other women dealt with their lives resourcefully when confronted with difficult circumstances. With her zest and optimism never diminishing she was ready to face any obstacle.

Now for the three marriages. It takes a deep-down, romantic idealist head-in-the-clouds person to go up to the altar and say "I do" three times and mean it. Of all the "isms" a person can accrue, her ideal-ism topped the list, creating trouble and sometimes delight in her life. The wisdom obtained from all this was to keep on going never quitting until everything felt close to perfect.

With the first "I do", she was extremely young, naïve, inexperienced in the ways of the world longing for a family, husband, children, a house surrounded by flowers, a dreamy situation. Suddenly Mr. "Almost Right" appeared out of the blue! He was a clean cut, handsome Naval Officer from a foreign nation. A quiet man with enigmatic behavior, misinterpreted as good reasoning by her folks, especially her grandfather. This young fellow was a man of very few words, an easy assignment, especially in a foreign country. He had no aspirations of learning her native language, and she spoke his effortlessly. Approval by her family was immediate and enthusiastic. They all hoped that this union would be a source of taming her down a bit from her rebellious, zany, impractical, cockamamie, impulsive ways. Fortunately or not, it didn't happen. He didn't restrain her, and she didn't ignite him either. A small example, she loved music and dancing; he never heard of the word rhythm, it was not part of his nature. The cultural differences were insurmountable. He was from a little town in one country, and she from a large urban area of another. Intellectually and geographically they were oceans apart. He turned out to be an unimaginative, stern, overly cautious to the point of distrust, no "joie de vivre", no dreams of the future, unenthusiastic about everything, all in all a no-pleasure-at-any-cost kind of person. They were opposites in every aspect. She had hoped that he would grow and change and that they sooner or later would merge. Other couples she saw around them seemed to be bored with each other. So she consoled herself with the thought that this might be the normal way for married people. Amazingly enough, this mismatch lasted over twenty years and they were blessed with two appealing children, a girl and a boy.

Back in those days there was no marriage counseling. Even if there had been, their situation was beyond mending. Nothing would have helped. The dissimilarities were too great. There was no tangible reason for a divorce. It all just came to a quiet closure. She could not stand their lives together anymore, not another day, not another minute. She divorced him. Older Navy wives had pointed to her as the perfect example of the loyal "little woman" who stood on the pier, smiling and waving to her husband as he left for long trips, then went home to take care of the nest with great dedication. The truth was that she was glad to see him leave, her chance for being carefree again. She and the children could have lots of jolly times doing all the things that they would not do when Daddy was around. To this day, decades afterwards, she recalls saying to the kids as they all jumped and danced around in the living room, "Time to stop having fun, here comes Daddy" as he drove up to the front of their house.

Couples who broke up were stigmatized and ostracized during that era. They were looked on as having a total lack of morals and unable to work out the "for-better-or-for-worse" when the going got worse. Criticism, brought on by misinformed sources, was rampant, especially aimed at the wife. Once again she became a single mother after having been one for many years during her husband's absences on long naval trips to sea as part of his career.

Unhappily married ladies in the neighborhood who didn't have the courage to follow the example set by this intrepid young woman were filled with envy and entertained themselves by gossiping. This mother of two active kids went through an extremely difficult stage in life. She was lonely in her plight, worried, scared and treated unfairly by her peers who accused her of wrong doing as she suffered deep pain. The same ones that called her the "exemplary Navy wife" were now accusing her of being the "perfectly fake one". Vulnerable and anxious to lead a conventional existence, she endured great stress crying herself to sleep many a night emotionally exhausted.

At a time like that she was easy prey for what might have seemed like a miraculous solution. Down the road he came into view one day. It was a simple, almost effortless way out of this disheartening situation. She fell into this second marriage mainly as relief from her difficult plight. Of course he was personable, charming, a great dancer, loved having fun, with flawless manners and adored her children. What more could she want? He not only captured her but the kids as well, playing games with them and often bringing treats. "Playing games" suited him, as he was an expert at it…turning out to exercise the technique of a first class gigolo. Of course who would have imagined such a thing? They were all caught in the lure of this guy who came out of nowhere and seemed to be the answer to end all questions! This lonely single mother of two fell right in "hook, line and sinker"…and off to the altar they went (after he finally was able to have a blood test without fainting…this could have a been a kind of omen, but taken lightly during the excitement of the moment).

They were married for a short time, just a few months, when he merrily made the following statement to her: "With the monthly allowance I get from my dad, the current salary from your job and the child support sent to you by your ex, I simply don't have to concern myself with looking for employment. I'll just enjoy a relaxed stress free life." This statement left her speechless! Her reaction was total disbelief and shock. Following this traumatic declaration and after some thinking she looked for an attorney to see about the possibility of an annulment… This husband was a pathetic looser dressed up in charisma attire. It was not possible to annul the marriage; he would not admit to his ways or sign a anything. He was much too comfortable and happy. After all why should he give up this snug arrangement? The only recourse left to her was to file for a divorce, on the obvious grounds of his actions. By now she knew how, and the process was not as difficult or as hurtful as before. She just felt stupid and gullible. They had been living in her house. Following much conflict, the paper work was completed and sealed, the divorce lawyer advised her to toss him out of her property. She promptly did!

One unusual, somewhat amusing fact was that weeks later the ex wife of this opportunist, called the more recent divorcee, inviting her to lunch and confessed that she had wanted to warn the new bride about what could have happened but didn't think that her admonition would be credible under the circumstances.

She found herself once more the single mother of two, facing the world, struggling to make a living and keeping watch on the active youngsters. In her heart she wanted a family unit and all that goes with it. But up to then Fate had not blessed her with such dreams. An idealist still hoping that the best was yet to happen, she had to start building castles again and adopt new visions for the future. Her buoyancy had a nagging way of never leaving. After a few years of working in airlines, hotels and country clubs, she spotted an ad in the local newspaper about courses in hotel management. They were offered by a well known university specializing in the hospitality business. The school was not far and the classes were in the evening. She signed up for a series of them with an eye towards enhancing her knowledge and progressing in that field. After several weeks of instruction she became acquainted with one of the students, and they struck a friendship through their common interests. After classes they would go out for coffee and lively discussions. He was an outgoing sophisticated person, they "hit it off" quickly and the casual friendship soon began to shape into a deeper connection. They shared similar plans for the future in the hotel world. Some time passed and she took him home to meet the children. He was sweet and friendly to them. Immediate rapport was established. She turned into melted butter when someone showed affection for her kids. Months later they became increasingly fond of each other and one evening over coffee and class revision he asked her to marry him. She accepted. A person crazy about her little family was worthy of another trip down the aisle and off to the altar they went. His second marriage, her third. Her incurable optimism prevailed again!

Unfortunately this couple's destiny was not written in the stars. It navigated through some pretty stormy seas for reasons that were difficult if not impossible to explain. He carried a heavy burden of guilt for having divorced his previous wife on the grounds of her mental instability and alcoholism. His adult children were not ready to accept their father's second spouse. Nowadays this would have been a marriage counselor's challenging case but they still were not easily available during the "stick to it or you are a miserable failure" era. The matrimony was heading for trouble but her resilience was still alive and kicking. Her mind set was to keep confronting destiny in her ever lasting quest for perfection. Why not? Another failure a new chance to begin again! She had not expected to drop into a puffy cloud of perfect bliss, just longed for a partner, a friend, a confidant, a supportive person, someone to share feelings, through thick or thin moments that are bound to happen in anyone's lifetime. This did not happen. He also had a problem with alcohol and during the drunken moments often became verbally abusive, accusing her of "practicing for widowhood" the instant she displayed a little self confidence. She shed many tears over these unkind remarks until the day when she decided that a little "practice" would not be such a terrible idea after all, making some adjustments in that direction. They were together for almost thirty years, never quite hearing the same melody. Their symphony ended on a somber note. Providence took over. After an extended illness he died, taking away with him all the nervous tension and unhappiness of both.

Along with his departure, her dreams quieted down along with them the hopes of happiness with a partner. By that time she had done a lot of surviving, and her thoughts took on a more realistic turn. Single-handed at the helm again for different reasons this time, navigating over the seas of life with a lot more experience, the same person as before, buoyant, lively, filled with the idea that going solo with only her viewpoint to be considered was as idyllic as it was going to get. She was foot loose, not fancy but utterly free. She could do whatever she wanted any time of the day or night, and no one had a say-so about her actions. This stage in her life was referred to as "wow wee wowzie lah dee dah halleluya" independence. This lack of restrictions was delightful, requiring some acclimating but did it ever feel good! No more squabbles, verbal abuse, tears, unhappy times feeling out of the loop with the in laws. Peace and freedom reigned. Contrary to the old maxim, one could live more cheaply than two....plus one added benefit was the absence of discord! Was this widow bereaved or relieved? Easy answer to figure out, isn't it?

Whose Choice Is It?

If you could arrange your first encounter with the person of your dreams, your life mate, your matching spirit, just where would it be? Which landscape would you choose? A balmy beach with faint murmurs of the ocean waves rolling in and out, gently caressing the sands and humming a tune heard only by the two of you? Or perhaps a library filled with shelves of books saturated with knowledge of things past and present? Would a tranquil park appeal to you, amidst the trees, flowers, with soothing echoes of nature and breezes smelling of green?

This couple did not meet under such idyllic conditions, enchanting as they might have been. The first glimpse they had of each other was a spot where romance usually doesn't thrive…the controlled atmosphere of a scientific laboratory. There was no particular immediate attraction between the two. Their relationship started as a friendly though detached sharing of common interests. No sounds of waves ebbing in and out, nor gentle breezes twirling in the air or nature fragrances of any colors. The outdoors was not involved in it at all. It was simply an academic environment, no emotions in attendance. The unexplainable made its grand entrance much later in the scene. Months passed as they went on exchanging views, debating theories late into the evenings, pouring over books until one night, oh yes, quite late, the alliance progressed into the "I can't live without you" phase. Cupid had arrived after a long flight across campus. One moment led into the next which progressed into engagement followed by marriage.

Twenty years of bliss, two sons, a closely knit family managing life's ups and downs, finances, schooling for the boys, career plans, aging together, retirement, buying a house overlooking the ocean, dreams of a brilliant future. The possibilities sparkled ahead making the every day occurrences and difficult moments a little easier to bear and gave them purpose and anticipation. Then one fateful day, the unforeseen came tumbling into their lives. After a medical check-up, her husband arrived home brimming with the joy of perfect health, filled with optimism, ready for anything. He dashed up to his studio to work on some papers. After a little while the whole house seemed enveloped in an ominous silence followed by a loud thump coming from upstairs. She ran up as fast as she could to find him on the floor lifeless.

The doctors told her later that he had suffered a massive heart attack, killing him instantaneously. He was fifty one years old with a lot of living to do and many prospects for a dazzling future. Everything vanished way in one inexplicable moment. She stood there looking down at him in complete disbelief, emotionally paralyzed, not knowing what to do. Who could explain such an incident? What would happen next? How would she tell the boys when they came back from school? What would life be like in his absence? Was this plan designed by a larger than life force? His days were finished; hers were at a standstill. Life came to a stop for the entire family. She found herself heartbroken, lonely, worried, isolated, a single mother of two adolescent boys with all the hurdles of boyhood to manhood coming around the corner. She had to keep the days going as smoothly as possible. Living was bleak. This was a preface to a new kind of survival, the emotional one. Everything started all over again except that this time she was the only one in charge. She embarked on this new voyage with the full experience of the past to confront an uncertain future. Courage was now needed more than ever.

Reflections on widowhood: Contentment or unhappiness are in large measure part of your own mission. Blaming others will not make anything happen or go away. It is up to you to generate enchantment without the magic wand. Some efforts bear fruit, some will get you nowhere. Support groups of older or younger women don't always help, they pigeonhole you in a category and that does not fit you. What might make life easier for you is self-observation. Eventually you will arrive at a place that clearly defines you, and then progress begins to take shape. The ramp onto the major highway of existence is in sight. Take it even if you don't have a map, just keep on driving!

Traveling was something she always dreamed about but it was not her husband's preference. When he was alive, the children were small and the budget tight so they didn't go anywhere. Now as a widow with children grown up, there were many singles groups to join and see the world. You don't have to go alone and it's much more fun in the company of others. You meet interesting people who travel for a variety of reasons besides just seeing new places. New friendships, companionships and relationships crop up from it.

As for finances, get professional help whether you have a little or a lot you may need assistance in handling your investments. It's essential to be money smart and not allow your resources to get out of control.

Single parenthood has its pluses and minuses. You are responsible for all decisions. If something goes right, you get the rewards. If something goes wrong, you're fully to blame. The loss of a parent is traumatic for children, and their reaction will vary depending on the child. They look to you for moral and emotional support, even when you need assistance yourself. If grandparents are nearby that's helpful too when the going gets overwhelming for just one parent.

Dating again…???? Prince Charming is not going to land at your door step, especially if you have two kids. It's possible to meet a diversity of people in church activities, clubs, gyms lectures, sport events etc. These places attract persons of similar interests…worth a try.

Finally and of utmost importance, take care of yourself, your personal appearance, your health. After years of being too busy with home, children, and family, you may have neglected your self needs. Get in shape, exercise your body and your options! Live while you're alive!

Death of a Marriage

After a few years as a single mother with children to raise, she decided to join a widow's group and relate to others in similar situations to see what was out there and how people were dealing with their lives. Did everyone else have the same dark moments? Was anybody leading a desolate, lonely life just as she was? Were they surviving by floating in their own ocean of sorrows? Were there ways of being content going along with their fate being reasonably happy? If so, how? She made up her mind to find the answers to these questions. When she wasn't running around chasing kids or chauffeuring them to school and other activities, her life was a haze of solitude as though she were the only widow in the world.

Following much reflection, she sought a way out of this isolation towards a better life. There had to be a way. She was going to pursue it till she found it, determined to embrace it and revolutionize her existence!

The rest of this narrative is not a fairly tale. There is no happy ending, just an end…which in an astringent way could pass for "happy", but not as we normally think of it. In an attempt to find a better way she staggered into the worst. At one of those group encounters she met the affliction that would follow her for a decade of pure distress—her second husband. The dream boat turned out to be the shipwreck of her life. A charming, outgoing, sociable type of guy who met everyone with a smile, dressed in a crisp Navy officer's uniform. She admits that she was an easy target for the military maneuvers and quickly sank for his attention disguised as affection. Some call it chemistry, electricity, magnetism. Whatever the label, she got an acute case of falling-in-love-head-over-heels for this dapper man, heading for destruction of her self esteem and confidence in her own judgment.

After a short courtship, they married. That's when her difficulties began. For starters, the eve of their wedding, her parents were in town for the occasion staying at a local hotel. She, the glowing bride wanted to go see them one more time to show them how happy she was with dreams of a future with Prince Charming. The groom opposed the idea and would not allow her to go, expressing his feelings in an abusive manner by pushing her around and banging her head against the wall while yelling "no!" It was so frightening that for a instant she considered running away from the idea, canceling the ceremony. Yet her buoyant self thought no, it was just the excitement of the moment. The first severe mistake by both! He, for the terrible treatment of a woman about to be his wife, and she, for not following her instinct of scurrying in the other direction as fast and as far from him as possible. From then on it was uphill hill and stormy all the way. He brought to this marriage four children by a previous wife, and she had two adopted of her own. Altogether a handful of little ones, the oldest being twelve. Her life was a constant race preparing meals, doing laundry, taking them to school, picking them up from various children's groups with an assortment of schedules. All the while she endured maltreatment from this man, adding to this her full-time job outside the home. For some inexplicable reason, he was particularly physically abusive towards her and her son, more than to the others. To this day, more than thirty years later she wonders why and how she endured that life. She was unable to assess her own feelings at that time. Her mind became deadened to logical thinking, incapable of struggling for her emotional well-being. She was too busy and humiliated to have a moment's clarity to somehow escape this torment. He made sure that she could not get away by totally controlling her and the children. They were all helpless under his power. One day he decided that they should move into the country and live in tents for a while, to expose the children to nature and have them learn survival. She had to home school all six children so they would not be influenced by the outside world and other children's companionship and ideas. At that point she had to give up her outside employment, thereby becoming even more dependent on him. His motives were beyond human comprehension. The whole family were captives of this tyrant who ruled with an iron fist, with uncontrollable rage and manipulating the family into a downward spiral. He managed to convince her that she was beneath him in every way with no capability of ever existing without his stern guidance and harsh punishment to guide her towards the correct course of life.

Through a mysteriously devious motive, she got him to agree to attend sessions with a marriage therapist and see what could be done to improve their situation which he attributed completely to his wife's erroneous attitude concerning everything. She was hopeful that a counselor would lead them into a non-violent direction. It did not happen. The husband turned on his charm, methodically enthralling the analyst into agreeing that the whole problem was due to the wife's inability to see reality in a clear light and deal with the every day ups and downs which are bound to happen in any marriage. The wife was by now convinced that she indeed was a "basket case" trapped in a tunnel of misery without the slightest glimpse of a light at either end.

They returned to their usual day-to-day routine when things got even worse. He suddenly made another dismal announcement. He would build a one-room shack in the woods for the two of them, with the children staying under tents communing with nature, learning to toughen up in any kind of weather while the two of them had the "luxury" of this shed without running water or any of the most basic facilities. She had to prepare meals over a wood fire and wash clothes in the river where she and the children also bathed.

Gradually she developed an unwholesome attachment to this man—probably resulting from a brutal form of mind control, much as some prisoners have for their captors. She persuaded herself that she could never really succeed at anything and was incapable of making reasonable decisions…as she endured inhumane treatment or was made to observe all the children verbally and or physically battered.

Despite all this, she made another valiant attempt at seeking help, this time from a psychiatrist. Her husband went along knowing that he would once again substantiate his wife's weaknesses to a professional. The doctor, after a few consultations, came to the unmistaken conclusion that the husband needed deep psychological intervention and ordered him interned into an anger management facility for long term treatment.

At last, the beginning of the end came into view! The nightmare was nearly over. She was able to divorce him on grounds of extreme cruelty and was granted custody of all six children. He was legally bound through his military pay to send child support and alimony for as long as required by law.

This unsinkable, courageous woman recovered her astonishing zest for life, a gusto that had been dormant for all those years and began to breathe freely again. The children had acquired an enormous respect and admiration for their "mom", for her strength and love for others. As the kids got older, she returned to her job at a local business in charge of their accounting department where she remained for several years.

By the time I had the honor and privilege of interviewing this remarkable human being she struck me as the happiest individual that ever lived on earth—full of joy, humor, dreams, plan, with the enviable energy and enthusiasm of the eternal child enchanted with the world and everything in it. Feet on the ground and head in the stars…an admirable person, a true survivor! Her past was placed exactly where it belonged—behind her; the future, a dazzling one, was waiting ahead on the map of her travels to magical lands far away.

A marriage died, but a life was born ready to discover a new magnificent world! At the beginning of this story I mentioned that the ending was not happy…now I'm delighted to admit…I was wrong!

Annex

1. Questionnaire used as basis for interviews
2. How did you meet your husband?
3. What was the initial attraction?
4. How long were you married?
5. Was your marriage happy? Or not?
6. Did your husband die from a long illness?
7. Did he die suddenly?
8. How did you feel right away? Shock, anger, disbelief, or some other emotion?
9. Was it a form of distress or relief?
10. How did you handle grief?
11. What did you miss most about being married?
12. Did you begin planning your future as a single person? Something you had always wanted to do because of being married, family, children?
13. What was most difficult to face?
14. What helped?
15. What did not help?

16. What is good in your life now?

17. Did you change your lifestyle, have a career in mind, decide to do something of your own?

18. Did you consider remarrying?

19. What would you do again in life? What are your regrets, if any?

20. What are your reflections on widowhood?

21. What advice would you have for new widows?